AROUND TOWN

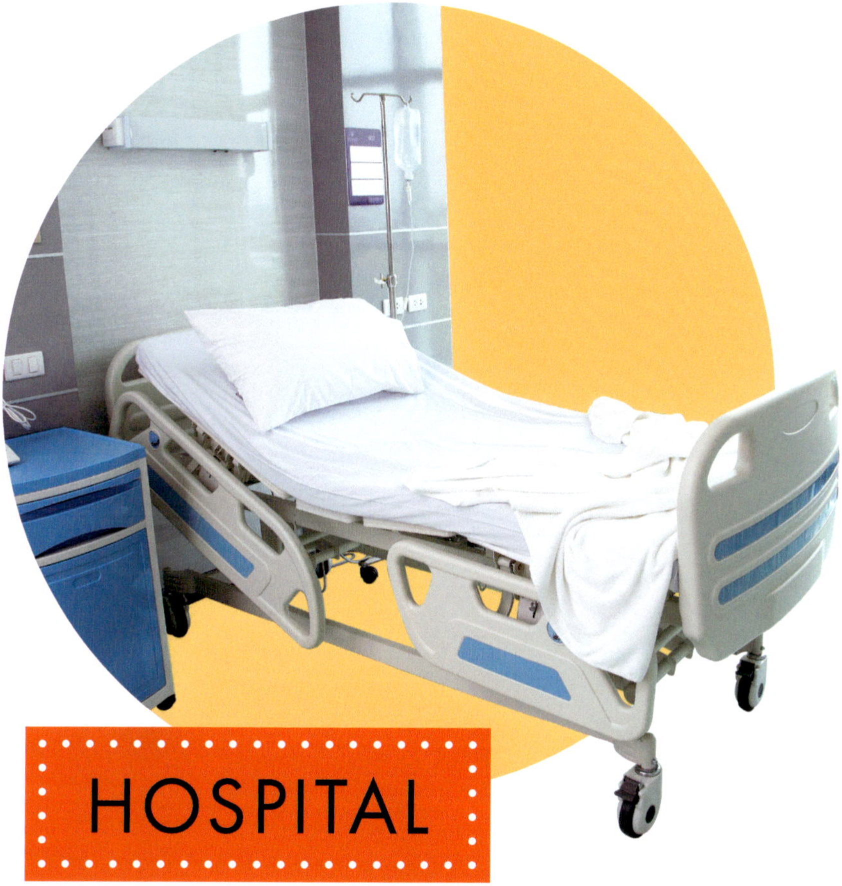

HOSPITAL

by Susan Rose Simms

ambulance

IV

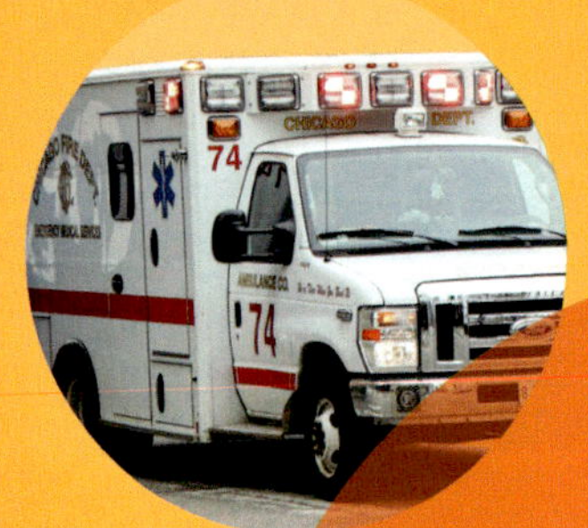

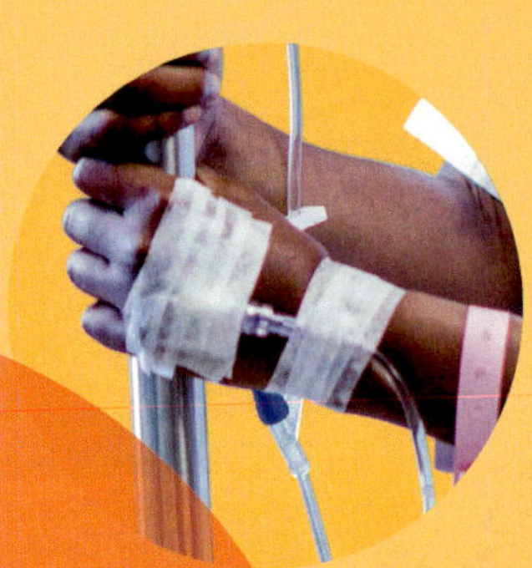

Look for these words and pictures as you read.

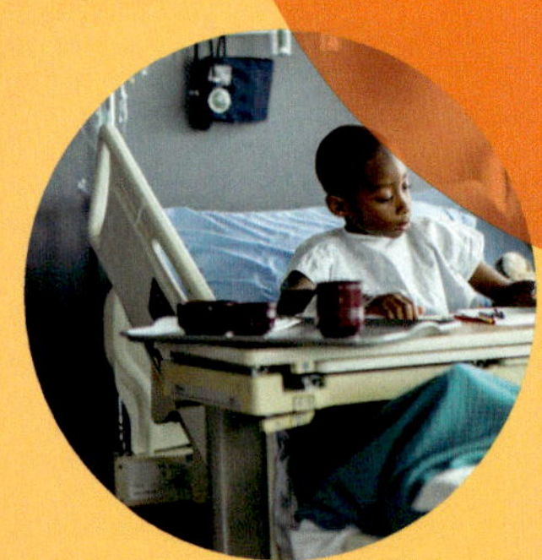

bed

gown

Let's go visit the hospital.
What will we see?

CHICAGO
74
CHICAGO FIRE DEPT.
EMERGENCY MEDICAL SERVICES
AMBULANCE CO.
We're There When You Need Us
74

Look at the ambulance.
It goes to the hospital.
It's fast!

ambulance

Look at the surgeon.
He is a doctor.
He helps people
by doing operations.

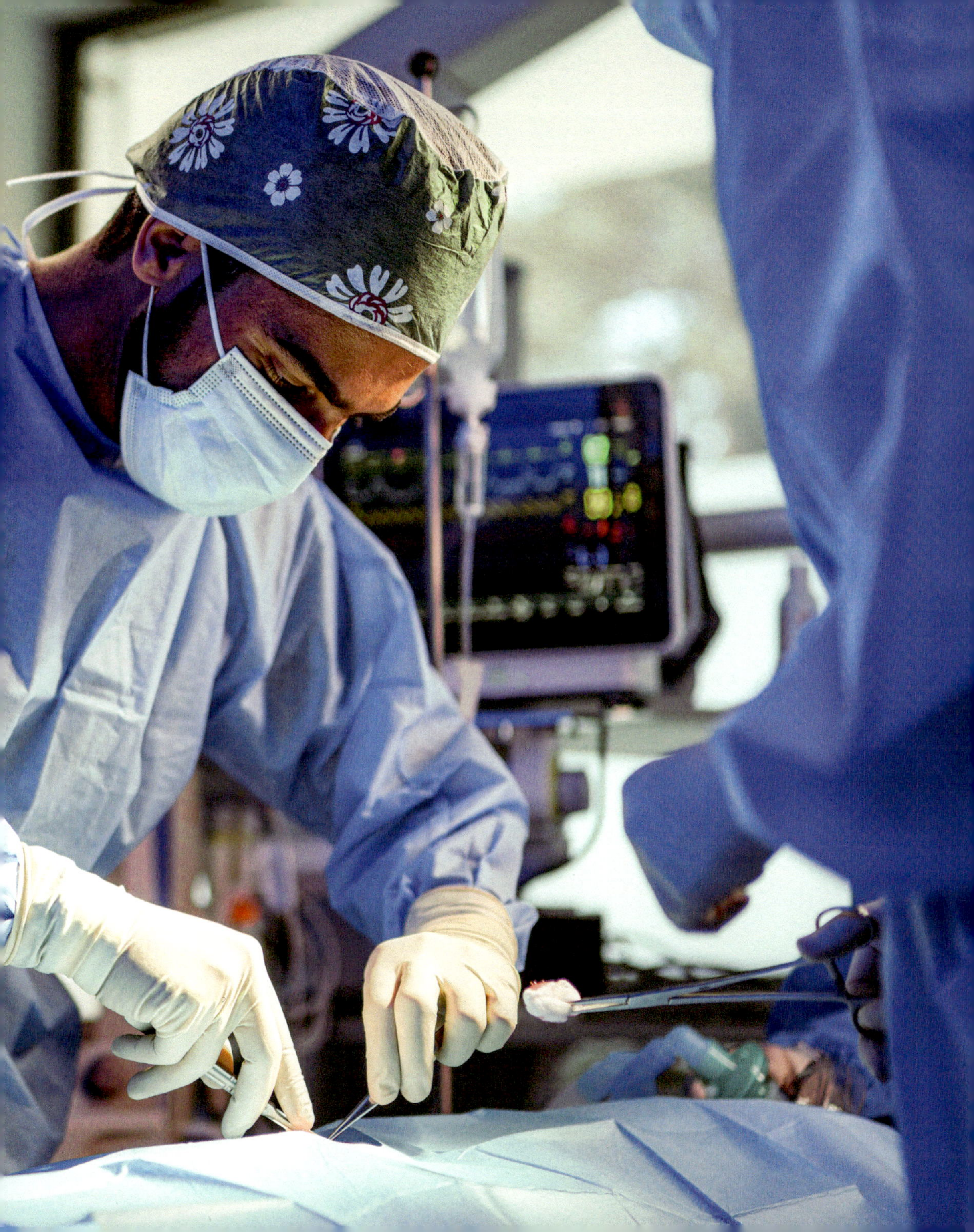

Look at the IV.
It is a tiny tube for medicine.
It goes in Kira's arm.

bed

Look at the bed.
It has sides.
They keep Ken safe.

gown

Look at the gown.

Tie it in the back.

It keeps you covered.

Hospitals never close. They help people day and night.

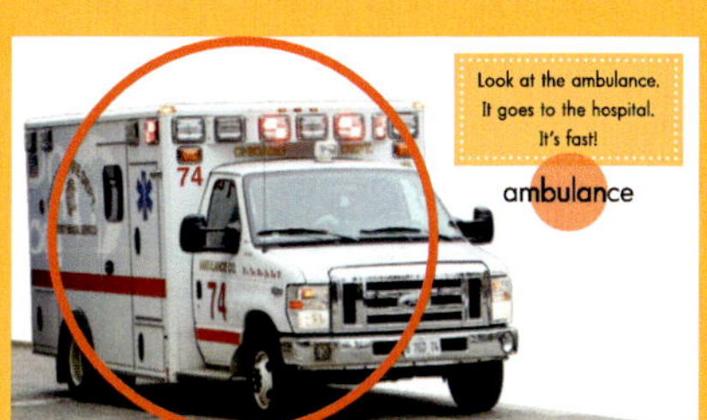

ambulance

IV

Did you find?

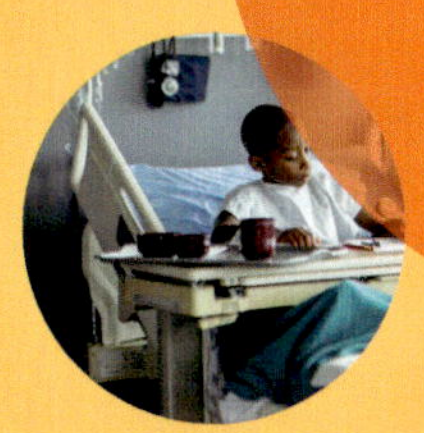

bed

gown

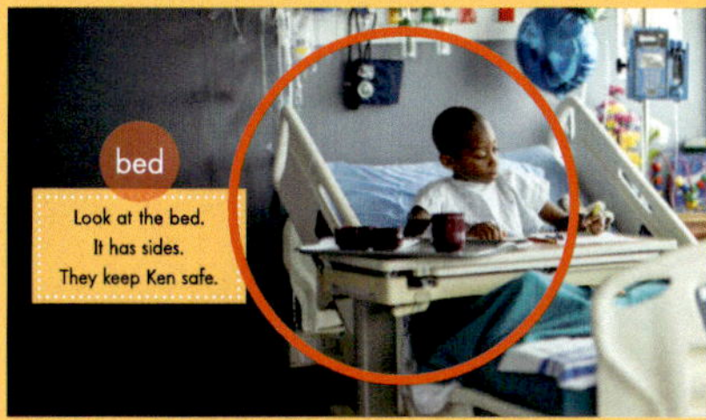

Spot is published by Amicus Learning, an imprint of Amicus
P.O. Box 227, Mankato, MN 56002
www.amicuspublishing.us

Cataloging-in-Publication data is available
from the Library of Congress.
Library Binding ISBN: 9798892008273
Paperback ISBN: 9798892008938
eBook ISBN: 9798892009591

LCCN: 2025012839

Ana Brauer, editor
Deb Miner, series designer
Sara Hood, book designer
and photo researcher

Photos by Getty Images/andresr, 3, FatCamera, 2, 10–11, 15, FS Productions, 2, 12–13, 15, Halfpoint Images, 6–7, JazzIRT, 14; Shutterstock/ BigPixel Photo, 1, Leonard Zhukovsky, 2, 4–5, 15, SocoXbreed, cover, 16, wavebreakmedia, 2, 8, 15